omething but to be someone. Fashion *[is unique to]*

e must always be different. There are people who

comfortable; othe*rwise it is* not luxury. Fashion

tion! One cannot be forever innovating. I want to

think for yourself. Aloud. A fashion that does not

ne loses when one decides not to be something but to

In order to be irreplaceable one must always be

le who are rich. Luxury must be comfortable;

To my son, Gabe

First edition 2007

Library of Congress Cataloging-in-Publication Data

Matthews, Elizabeth.
Different like Coco / Elizabeth Matthews. — 1st ed.
p.   cm.
ISBN 978-0-7636-2548-1
1. Chanel, Coco, 1883–1971 — Juvenile literature. 2. Women fashion designers — France — Biography — Juvenile literature. 3. Fashion design — France — History — 20th century — Juvenile literature. I. Title.
TT505.C45M38 2007
746.9'2092 — dc22
[B]   2006040622

09 10 11 12 13 14 TWP 10 9 8 7 6

Printed in Singapore

This book was typeset in Bernhard Modern and Futura.
The illustrations were done in pen and ink.

Candlewick Press
99 Dover Street
Somerville, Massachusetts 02144

visit us at www.candlewick.com

Different Like Coco

ELIZABETH MATTHEWS

CANDLEWICK PRESS

AT A TIME when France was the center of all that was wealthy, grandiose, and fashionable, Gabrielle "Coco" Chanel was born poor and skinny.

COCO WAS ALWAYS DIFFERENT.

Her family lived in a one-room house, her mother struggled with failing health, and her father, a street merchant, often traveled. Coco sometimes accompanied her father to the marketplace, where he sold hats, aprons, and clothes.

The wealthy ladies of society strolled elegantly around the stands, their faces glowing beneath partly drawn veils and their hands clutching packages filled to the brim with the most expensive finery in all of France.

Though she had five brothers and sisters, Coco preferred to play alone. Retreating to her imaginary world, she could pretend to live like the ladies she saw at the market.

"Merci, mademoiselle, I got this hat this very afternoon."

"Oui. They are the height of fashion. I got the very last one. I told Monsieur that I absolutely must have the black one with the veil. It's so much more dramatic."

When Coco was twelve, her mother died. Her brothers were sent to work at a neighboring farm. Coco and her two sisters were sent to an orphanage in Auvergne.

Cold and colorless, the orphanage rested among medieval ruins in a gorge, surrounded by a forest of trees.

At the convent, life was disciplined. Aging nuns in pressed habits gave the girls strict lessons in reading and writing. All was clean and simple, black and white.

It was at the convent that Coco learned to sew. Out of scraps of fabric, she made rag dolls and ribbons for her hair. Her talent with a needle and thread made the dolls beautiful. Her famous imagination brought them to life.

Coco fantasized about living with family again. She imagined herself dressed in elegant gowns and owning thoroughbred horses. Mostly she fantasized that she would one day be adored by the society that now looked down its nose at her because she was penniless.

She always believed she deserved more. She loved to read cheap romance novels and rarely told the truth. She constantly rearranged and romanticized the facts of her life story. She would even tell lies in confession!

At eighteen, Coco was sent to Notre Dame, a finishing school for young ladies in Moulins. As a charity case, she lived with other indigent girls in an unheated dormitory. In classes and at meals, they were made to sit apart from the paying students and to eat second-rate food.

Despite the overwhelming and humiliating distinction drawn between rich and poor at Notre Dame, Coco learned to carry herself with as much pride and elegance as the wealthiest young ladies. She studied their neatly polished shoes and even more polished manners, and matched them from her confident posture all the way up to her arrogant smile.

In the early 1900s, many considered it socially unacceptable for a woman to work. Those few who had to work or chose to work were permitted to enter only a handful of occupations, such as nursing, tailoring, or domestic service. When Coco left Notre Dame, she gladly joined a tailoring shop, determined to use her sewing skills to realize her aspirations for success.

Coco couldn't afford to dress like the corseted ladies of high society, and she was never going to be shapely. There was no point in trying to be just like them. Instead, she tried to be different.

She started making her own hats, but didn't stop there. Arrogantly simple, her designs shocked everyone.

At twenty-one, Coco sneaked into her first polo match and was hooked. The racetrack was the center of the Parisian social scene. Every day she could mingle with the most prestigious people in all of France. It was at the racetrack that she met Arthur "Boy" Capel, a wealthy British aristocrat and famous polo player.

It was love at first sight, though they would never marry.
In the early 1900s, a family's social standing meant everything,
and Coco didn't come from a "respectable" family. Nevertheless,
Boy Capel loved her and her rebellious ideas.

"My love, what can
I get you? Diamonds?
Emeralds?"

"No, no, *monsieur*,
you needn't get
me anything
except . . . my
own little shop
in Paris."

He bought her a small shop, just as she wished,
on *la rue* Cambon, one of the most fashionable streets
in Paris.

She gave it a small white awning and had her
name painted in black letters across it.

Coco designed and sold only clothes that *she* wanted to wear. They were practical, long, and slender, and there were absolutely no corsets.

Coco could not draw, so she designed by laying the fabric over wooden dummies or on models who would stand patiently while she sewed.

In order to create a sense of mystery, Coco would hide and work in the back of her shop. From there, she could watch the reactions of customers to her daring designs and even more daring prices.

Her style was like nothing anyone had ever seen. It was so unpredictable and simple, but everyone loved it.

One breezy afternoon, Coco borrowed one of Boy's jersey sweaters. To avoid pulling it down over her neatly coifed hair, she cut it down the front, added ribbon to the edges, and finished it with a collar and a bow. Her reinvented sweater was a huge success. Coco had created a new look, that of the modern sportswoman.

"She has more sense than any other woman in Europe."
—Pablo Picasso

"Until now, women were beautiful and architectural, like the prow of a ship. Now they resemble undernourished telephone operators."
—Paul Poiret

In 1914, World War I was brewing and Germany invaded France. With the draft calling all the men to war, women had to work. It was impossible to work in a corseted gown, but Coco's designs were perfect. While other Paris businesses were failing, Coco's was thriving. The streets were filled with her simple dark designs, worn by the new working class as well as by widows in mourning.

In 1915, Coco opened another shop. By 1916, she had a staff of three hundred. In her studio, she often wore long strings of pearls from which a pair of scissors hung, ready to rip out any ill-fitting seams. Dramatic and exacting, she demanded perfection.

The war in full swing brought a rationing of cloth.
The press instructed women to lose weight so
that less material would be used to make
their dresses. With the textile industry
collapsing, Coco was able to get large
amounts of jersey inexpensively.
Consequently, many of her designs
were unflattering to a full figure.

After the war, fashion became
even more directed to a new kind
of woman, one who was athletic
and agile—one who was young
and slender like Coco.

Women no longer wanted just to dress like Coco—they wanted to *be* just like Coco. Her distinctive beauty lay in an attitude, something that even the richest of socialites couldn't buy.

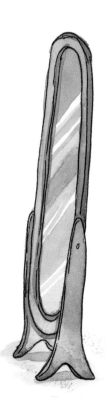

Upper-class society didn't usually socialize with common working people, but Coco changed all that. She treated her wealthy clients as her equals and demanded to be treated as their equal in return. This daring challenge to the established social order lifted Coco Chanel above the rank of mere seamstress to a creator of Parisian couture. Coco offered women not only freedom from corsets, but freedom from social constraints as well.

Nothing could attract more attention to Coco than just being herself. Her striking red lips, her energy, her style, and her boldness made her an instant celebrity.

EVERYONE LOVED COCO.
AND SHE WAS ALWAYS
DIFFERENT.

FASHION TIME LINE

1904   Coco Chanel takes a job at a tailoring shop.

1910   Coco sets up a millinery shop in Paris.

1913   Coco opens her first dress shop, on *la rue* Cambon in Paris.

1915   She opens a second shop.

1921   The eponymous perfume, Chanel No. 5, debuts. It contained more than eighty ingredients and was the world's most expensive perfume at the time.

Coco Chanel develops her signature cardigan jacket.

1923   Coco designs stage costumes for the play *Antigone*.
She goes on to design stage costumes for other plays and film costumes for several movies.

1926   Searching for something to wear to the theater, Coco creates and debuts "the little black dress."

1931   Samuel Goldwyn pays Chanel one million dollars to dress some of his biggest stars, including Katharine Hepburn, Grace Kelly, Elizabeth Taylor, and Gloria Swanson.

1939   Coco Chanel closes all of her boutiques.

1954   A successful comeback restores Coco Chanel to the ranks of haute couture.

She introduces the pea jacket and bell-bottom pants for women.

1971   Coco Chanel dies.

Philippe Guibourgé takes over as head of the House of Chanel.

1983   Karl Lagerfeld becomes premier designer and head of the House of Chanel.

Among Coco Chanel's many other innovations and contributions to women's fashion during her lifetime: the tricot sailor frock, the pullover sweater, the jersey dress, gypsy skirts, embroidered blouses and shawls, the box jacket, the trench coat, pleated skirts, jumpers, turtleneck sweaters, the blazer, the sling pump, and strapless dresses.

BIBLIOGRAPHY

BOOKS

Baillén, Claude. *Chanel Solitaire.* New York: Quadrangle/New York Times, 1974.

De La Haye, Amy, and Shelley Tobin. *Chanel: The Couturiere at Work.* New York: Overlook, 1994.

Galante, Pierre. *Mademoiselle Chanel.* Chicago: Henry Regnery, 1973.

Madsen, Axel. *Chanel: A Woman of Her Own.* New York: Henry Holt, 1990.

Richards, Melissa. *Chanel: Key Collections.* London: Welcome Rain, 2000.

Wallach, Janet. *Chanel: Her Style and Her Life.* New York: Doubleday/Nan A. Talese, 1998.

Wiser, William. *The Crazy Years: Paris in the Twenties.* New York: Thames and Hudson, 1983.

INTERNET RESOURCE

Sischy, Ingrid. "Coco Chanel." *Time* 100 Profiles. *Time* Magazine. http://www.time.com/time100/artists/profile/chanel.html.

How many cares one loses when one decides not to become unfashionable. In order to be irreplaceab have money and people who are rich. Luxury mus is architecture: it is a matter of proportions. In create classics. The most courageous act is still reach the streets is not a fashion. How many car be someone. Fashion is made to become unfashiona different. There are people who have money and